C000078514

THE PERFECT LEADER

Andrew Leigh is the author of several successful books on decision making, management techniques and effective change, all published by the Institute of Personnel Management. He trained as an economist at LSE, has an MA in Manpower Studies from London University and is a Fellow of the IPM. He started his career in marketing, and was for several years a business writer including three years on the business section of *The Observer*. He was a practising senior manager in the public service for many years.

Michael Maynard has led business and management workshops across the UK and in Europe, specializing in creativity, self-expression, communication skills and careers. After receiving an honours degree in sociology from London University he has had a successful career in the performing and creative arts, and was a familiar face on TV. He led the acclaimed 'Mastery' course at the Actors Institute in the City of London, and has been a pioneer in using theatre techniques in education and business. He has written for radio and TV (including *Not the Nine O'Clock News*) and created many industrial training videos and audio-visual presentations.

Andrew Leigh and Michael Maynard run Maynard Leigh Associates, the management development and consultancy service. Many major organizations are MLA clients, including Allied Dunbar, The Body Shop, British Airways, Hilton, Ladbrokes, The Stock Exchange, Sun Life and Texas Home Care.

You can contact Maynard Leigh Associates for information about leadership skills training, Leading Your Team workshops and manuals and additional materials at

Marvic House
Bishops Road
London SW6 7AD
Tel: 0171 385 2588
Fax: 0171 381 4110

OTHER TITLES IN THE SERIES

THE
PERFECT
LEADER

All you need to get it right first time

Andrew Leigh and
Michael Maynard

RANDOM HOUSE
BUSINESS BOOKS

This edition published in the United Kingdom in 1999
by Random House Business Books

First published in 1996 by Arrow Books
Random House, 20 Vauxhall Bridge Road, London SW1V 2SA

Random House Australia (Pty) Limited
20 Alfred Street, Milsons Point
Sydney, New South Wales 2061, Australia

Random House New Zealand Limited
18 Poland Road, Glenfield
Auckland 10, New Zealand

Random House South Africa (Pty) Limited
Endulini, 5a Jubilee Road, Parktown 2193, South Africa

Random House UK Limited Reg. No. 954009

Papers used by Random House UK Limited are natural, recyclable
products made from wood grown in sustainable forests. The
manufacturing processes conform to the environmental regulations
of the country of origin.

ISBN 0 09 940622 5

Companies, institutions and other organizations wishing to make
bulk purchases of any business books published by Random House
should contact their local bookstore or Random House direct:
Special Sales Director
Random House, 20 Vauxhall Bridge Road, London SW1V 2SA

Tel: 0171 840 8470 Fax: 0171 828 6681

www.randomhouse.co.uk
businessbooks@randomhouse.co.uk

Typeset in Sabon by SX Composing DTP, Rayleigh, Essex
Printed and bound in Norway by AIT Trondheim AS

Contents

The 7 I's of Leadership

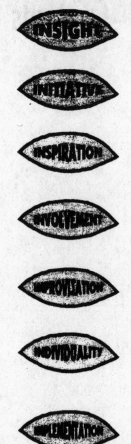

Leadership is in the I of the beholder

Introduction

Every few hours someone, somewhere publishes a paper on leadership. By now we must surely know what it takes to be an effective leader? Not a bit of it! Despite endless research and illustrious attempts stretching back to Machiavelli and beyond, there is still no consensus on exactly what leadership is, how to learn or hold on to it, or even how important it is.

With few reliable leadership rules, here is one hard fact: leaders are mainly recognized *after* certain actions have occurred. People tend to say with hindsight – 'that was leadership'.

So you can feel encouraged. We tend to know leadership only when we see it. Defining or describing it in advance, prompts endless debates about meaning. At its simplest, leadership is about achieving things with the support of others. At its most complicated, leadership is about a description of behaviour that few of us might expect to emulate.

Between these two extremes is the reality that leadership is essentially a special relationship between the person leading, and those who are led. The ability to build such a relationship and understand what will contribute to creating it, is what the *The Perfect Leader* is all about.

REALITY CHECK

In the early 1990s, the Brussels-based Management Centre Europe reviewed leadership amongst 600 senior managers, in companies often employing more than 10,000 people. It found leadership thin on the ground:

- Most (90%) thought business leaders should be able to build effective teams but only 43% said their boss could
- Most (84%) felt good leaders should be good listeners but only 47% said their boss was
- Only a quarter felt a business leader should be motivated by power but more than half said this is what drove their boss
- Only 8% believed a leader should be ruthless and around a quarter accused their boss of being just that

Decades of research find virtually no connection between experience and one's ultimate performance as a leader.

Research into the characteristics of admired leaders is rather more consistent. In the US for example, surveys repeated over more than six years show that people admire leaders who are:

HONEST, FORWARD LOOKING, INSPIRING AND COMPETENT

NEED

We often realize that leadership is missing, while remaining unsure who should provide it, or what kind it should be. Organizations with inadequate leadership may be well managed, yet still on the road to oblivion. Others with an excess of leadership may face conflict over goals, or be disintegrating from too much direction and insufficient management.

What, then, is the perfect leader or indeed perfect leadership? It is tempting to use the military to answer this, with successful campaigners from Alexander the Great to Montgomery. Or one can refer to politicians from Abraham Lincoln to Winston Churchill. Yet Rommel too was a conquering military leader, though ultimately defeated. Churchill was a failed peace-time leader and Britain's long-serving Mrs Thatcher lost power once circumstances changed.

On Field Marshal Montgomery: 'In defeat, indomitable; in victory insufferable; in NATO, thank God, invisible.'
  Winston Churchill

Bob Geldof briefly acquired world leadership, campaigning against poverty. For slightly longer Mr Gorbachev led the Soviet Empire before vanishing into near obscurity. Leaders in companies like IBM, General Motors, American Express and many others have also rapidly vanished from the scene once their particular brand of leading was no longer required.

There *are* no perfect leaders, unless you count dead ones. Being a leader does not make you suddenly perfect, nor do you have to be perfect to become one. There are even ineffective leaders who despite all the odds somehow survive. So what will it take for you to succeed?

You need to realize that:

• Leaders are made not born
• You need others to be a leader
• There is no need to be perfect

3

People with no previous experience have often begun behaving like a leader and triumphed. Annually thousands of others learn and begin exercising the basics of leadership, even if the basics themselves are constantly in dispute.

Nor do you have to wait until you reach a suitable position or high status before exercising your leadership skills. You can do it anywhere – in a team, at home, at the local residents association, at school, in the PTA or hobby society. Wherever there's a job to be done, you can draw on your natural energy and start practising leadership.

'If a man is called to be a street sweeper, he should sweep streets even as Michelangelo painted, or Beethoven composed music, or Shakespeare wrote poetry. He should sweep streets so well that all the hosts of heaven and earth will pause to say, here lived a great street sweeper, who did his job well.'
Martin Luther King

SUPPORTERS

You are never a leader in isolation. It is not only what you do that counts, how you behave, what orders you give. It is also how others choose to respond to you. No wonder that the Chinese philosopher Lao-Tzu advised: 'To lead people, walk behind them.'

An actor on stage playing a king seems regal only because other actors are prepared to behave as *if* he is the king. No amount of regal posturing does the trick. Other people must react to the person as their leader. This applies equally to you.

Everyone, including you, is a potential leader, though not necessarily permanently. When you propose an idea at work, you are 'taking the lead' even if briefly. When you say 'I'll do that' in response to something that needs doing, you are also 'leading'.

Informal leadership based on behaviour, rather than relying on a formal role, moves around, in a group of people, particularly in highly creative situations where ideas and energy are rapidly shared. Nowadays, organizations are more aware of the value of informal leadership and many are trying hard to encourage it.

Since being a leader depends on others and is never in isolation, there are important ingredients making leadership possible:

The person . . . the situation . . . timing . . .
other people

You can influence all of these to some extent.

People who make it possible for you to lead are sometimes described rather dismissively as 'followers'. This suggests passivity though, and underestimates how dependent you are on such people. They are more like supporters, or even constituents.

To lead, you do not need to be perfect. Our knack of idealizing leaders arises from our natural way of compressing the so-called great ones into a single powerful quality: Nelson's strategy, Gandhi's persistence, Luther King's vision, Florence Nightingale's commitment, Pankhurst's determination, Churchill's oratory, Mandela's forgiveness, Mother Teresa's compassion.

Without such qualities perhaps you can never be a leader. History shows it to be otherwise. Even great leaders are flawed and less than perfect. Their skill is in getting things done despite their limitations, often in totally unexpected ways.

CHARISMA

'Charisma becomes the undoing of leaders. It makes them inflexible, convinced of their own infallibility, unable to change.'
    Peter F. Drucker, Management Consultant and writer

The high profile of some leaders is often attributed to a semi-magical quality called charisma. This powerful force seems to allow them to shape events, rather than be shaped by them. We regard such leaders as personally responsible for what their followers do: Nelson at Trafalgar, ICI's turnaround by John Harvey-Jones, Anita Roddick creating Body Shop, Archie Norman's rescuing of Asda, Branson graduating from a record chain to running a successful airline.

No single characteristic such as charisma, courage, energy or foresight entirely explains why people will support a leader.

'A high-profile charismatic leader is definitely not required to successfully shape a visionary company.'
    James Collins and Jerry Porras, *Built to Last*

Some of the most significant chief executives in the history of lively and long-lasting successful companies have not had the personality traits of the typical high-profile, charismatic leader. In fact many such leaders are virtually unknown, outside their own organization or industry.

Trying to develop charisma as a way of ensuring your leadership is a perfectly natural desire. But it is not a panacea. It will not ensure you become or even stay a leader. Anyway, you may not need it to lead an organization successfully.

It is easy to confuse charisma with excellence in other key aspects of leading, such as having a superb vision, being brilliant at getting things done, having a great commitment to developing people. Often great leaders are a product of their organization, rather than the other way around.

LIKEABILITY

An opinion poll on Moses would have shown that his iron vision and determination were hated by many of his flock, yet they still followed him into the desert and out the other side. So you do not need to be totally likeable to succeed as a leader. Few effective ones expect to be universally liked.

Indeed taking the lead may make you thoroughly unpopular. People such as Alan Sugar of Amstrad, or Rupert Murdoch the media baron, for example, are hardly popular figures, even amongst many of their staff. Yet they undoubtedly lead. However, they probably do so *despite* their abrasive personalities or style, rather than because of it. Whether as a leader it is better to be loved or feared has never been resolved.

INTEGRITY

Caesar Borgia reformed his country, restoring order and obedience. Hitler built nationwide roads and ended unemployment. Both despots were cruel, charismatic and failed to respect the difference between ends and means. Both ultimately failed.

Leadership can be regarded as amoral, it merely exists or it does not. However, leadership that does not contribute to human happiness, or that ultimately fails because of its destructive tendencies, is not the focus of *The Perfect Leader*. We focus on leadership that contributes constructively to human happiness, earning wide respect and possessing integrity.

You will need to discover your own unique way of leading. Merely copying other leaders and their personalities is unlikely to make you sufficiently special to gain real supporters. To discover your special leadership abilities means being willing to keep learning and growing as a human being:

The best leaders know themselves and what they want

To summarize so far:

- Most leaders are made, not born
- You can learn to lead
- You are not a leader in isolation, there must be people willing to be led – supporters
- Leading means you may be respected, not necessarily liked
- You need to discover your own unique way of leading
- Leaders keep learning, growing, know themselves and what they want

PRACTICE

Few leaders always get it right first time. You learn to lead by continuously learning and adjusting to achieve your vision. Are you willing to keep learning and give yourself lots of practice? Only by trying things out will you discover what works for you as a leader. You can never assume that because some other leader has adopted some way of getting things done, it will automatically work for you too.

Practice is how we learn most things and leadership is no different. Be prepared to seek opportunities for practising your leadership in as many different settings as possible. Only through practice will you come to lead instinctively, taking the role effortlessly, almost without thinking.

'I believe we learn by practice. Whether it means to learn to dance by practising dancing or to learn to live by practising living, the principles are the same. In each, it is the performance of a dedicated precise set of acts, physical or intellectual, from which comes shape of achievement, a sense of one's being, a satisfaction of spirit. One becomes in some area an athlete of God.'
Martha Graham, dancer and teacher.

Practice is one of the most important ways you gain self-confidence as a leader. So, like a musician practising the scales, or an actor rehearsing lines, keep practising the 7 I's of leadership.

Leadership style
What kind of leadership style should you adopt? Maybe you should be a decisive, autocratic leader who brooks no opposition but gets amazing things done. Or perhaps you should be a quiet, consultative leader who never makes a move without fully involving everyone.

There is no 'should'. All leaders develop a personal style that is unique to them and you will have to do the same. However, certain trends are making it harder to be one kind of leader as opposed to another, and there is also some evidence that having only one style of leadership is too limiting. You need a whole repertoire of styles, which you may adopt for different circumstances.

The way organizations are moving for the foreseeable future suggests that the old style 'command and control' type leader is no longer so effective. This is because hierarchy is giving way to the idea of 'community' of shared interests and stakeholders.

New-style leadership is about facilitative, empowering relationships with those who might support a leader. In fact the relationship is mutually supportive, rather than dependent and subordinate. In productive work, effective leaders are not commanders and controllers, bosses and big shots. They are servers and supporters, partners and providers.

This newer form of leadership style unleashes much more :

- energy
- talent
- commitment

than commanding and controlling.

THE 7 I'S

From our work with hundreds of teams and many leaders we find seven basic principles of leadership – the 7 'I's.

- **Insight**
- **Initiative**
- **Inspiration**
- **Involvement**
- **Improvisation**

- **Individuality**
- **Implementation**

These have stood the test of time. Talk to any effective leader about how they do it and they soon start referring in some way to one or more of the 7 I's, though not necessarily using the identical words.

The 7 I's are a useful way of remembering the seven leadership principles. They also highlight perhaps the most powerful part of effective leadership:

The ability to see what is needed

Throughout the rest of this book we will keep returning to this essential quality – to practise the art of seeing, of discovering what those who would be led need 'at this moment'.

The 7 I's
of Leadership

- ✦ Self-awareness
- ✦ Understanding others
- ✦ Seeing the situation

CHAPTER 1

Insight

'Couldn't you see?' he screams, about to storm out of the meeting.

'See what?' you say, hopelessly looking around.

'You must be blind, not to have noticed what's happening around here.'

Many of us have probably experienced what it's like missing the obvious. Remarks like 'it was staring you in the face' or 'you couldn't see the wood for the trees' remind us of these sometimes humiliating experiences. Often it is only with hindsight that we realize the signs were all around us.

Insight is your ability to accurately see events, circumstances and people, making sense of them. Leaders are strong on insight. Although this can seem a mysterious quality, in essence most people can learn how to have it too.

Insight uses both sides of your brain. There is the part that thinks logically, and another part that is more intuitive. We tend to use one type of thinking at the expense of the other. If you are primarily a logical, systematic person, you can practise tapping into the part of your brain that relies on instinct, feeling and emotion.

'To practise means to perform in the face of obstacles, some act of vision, of faith, of desire. Practice is a means of inviting the perfection desired.'
Martha Graham, dancer and teacher

If you tend to rely heavily on your gut feeling and an intuitive sense of what to do next, you can learn to take advantage of your brain's analytical powers. Even if you are mainly instinctive, your brain still has an extraordinary ability to classify and break down information into smaller, more manageable chunks.

People, events and circumstances often appear chaotic or meaningless. For example, sometimes you perform at your best while at other times you feel sluggish. Why? The people in your team are behaving in a peculiar way. Why? A previously strong market position suddenly appears under threat. Why? Customers who used to love the service no longer seem enamoured with it. Why? Faced with such uncertainty and disarray, many of us simply give up, regarding the world as hopelessly confusing.

Insight is essential for interpreting apparently chaotic information. It allows us to 'read' the environment and where necessary relate it to a plan or form of action. This ability to interpret stems from developing your:

- Self-awareness
- Understanding of others
- Perception of situations

SELF-AWARENESS

Deliberately or otherwise, successful leaders develop considerable personal insight. Often they may not share this with anyone. Yet they are usually aware of what is happening in themselves and how it affects their outward behaviour. If you hate the idea of increasing your self-awareness, then perhaps you should reconsider whether you truly want to be a leader.

Self-awareness is about how you see yourself, understanding your personality, your strengths and weaknesses. It is also about knowing the difference between how you see yourself and how others see you.

For example, people sometimes imagine their accent or appearance is holding them back from attaining their potential as a leader. They tend to cling to this belief even though people around them may give them completely contradictory feedback: 'we love your accent'; 'we think you look like a leader'. Negative self-image is destructive and can hold you back.

'You can't lead a cavalry charge if you think you look funny on a horse.'
John Peers, President, Logical Machine Corporation

Genuine self-awareness comes gradually, rather than suddenly like switching on a light. Occasionally though, one might suddenly gain an entirely new perspective on the world. Self-aware people:

Keep looking at what they do and how they do it

Successful leaders know their leadership is always on the line, liable to vanish instantly. So, either consciously or unconsciously, they regularly check how they are performing. It is rather like actors or musicians wanting to know what the director, conductor or critic thinks about their performance.

Self-aware people are not mere navel gazers. They

15

simply make enough time to reflect, to occasionally pause and wonder what is going on inside themselves. This is hard in a world that seems to work by sound bites, instant communication and great pressure for results.

You become more self-aware by consciously exploring:

- What is driving you
- Your current feelings
- Your present attitudes
- How others around you are feeling and reacting

Self-awareness is different from being self-conscious. When you are highly self-conscious, it is hard to absorb anything that is not just about you, rather than other people. It stops you seeing what is happening around you. It's like the person at a dinner party who talks incessantly about their own life and then calls it to a halt saying, 'I've done all the talking. Why don't you just tell us . . . what you think of me?'

Increase your self-awareness through :

Being willing to accept new information about yourself, and your impact on people around you.

Where would you find such information? Obviously you do not have it right now. You have to deliberately go looking for it. It means you ask for feedback, seek people's opinions and enquire what they are thinking, maybe put yourself in uncomfortable situations to obtain the information you need.

Checking it out
There are innumerable ways to explore yourself and

who you are. The method matters less than the willingness to discover more about you. Many people though, shy away from any form of self-examination, any type of introspection. Such people seldom make good leaders.

Try developing a clearer picture of your own strengths and weaknesses by creating a sort of personal balance sheet. You can use this to explore how best to develop further and become a more complete person. Even writing down such a list is a useful start. You need never show it to anyone else.

Psychometric tests, or personality profiles, are also ways of gaining a new perspective on yourself. These may have many different purposes, for example, to clarify your preferred role in a team, your tendency to take instant action or time to reflect, whether you care more about people or things, whether you are introspective or an extrovert, how you prefer to learn and so on.

Self-aware people possess a natural curiosity about themselves. They keep pursuing questions such as:

- Why did I do that?
- What effect did I have?
- Why did that work?
- How could I do that better?
- What went wrong with what I did?
- That worked, how can I do it again?
- How did they react to what I said or did?
- How am I feeling right now?

Total feedback
Some companies now use 360-degree feedback in which colleagues, peers and subordinates give a colleague important information about his or her performance and behaviour. Federal Express, for instance, expects its

corporate leaders both to receive this kind of feedback and act on it.

Such feedback certainly increases personal awareness. You are forced to confront how others see you, rather than just how you see yourself. For example, suppose you believe that you value other people and treat them with respect. Three-sixty-degree feedback may reveal that those on the receiving end of your behaviour do not see it that way.

Internal cast

An enjoyable way of enhancing your self-awareness is by exploring your 'internal cast of characters'. We each have many different 'people' inside us: the achiever, the bully, the coward, the lover, the joker, the procrastinator, the doer, the enthusiast, the painter, the eccentric and so on. These influence how we behave and respond to the world.

To begin exploring your internal cast of characters, start thinking of how you have responded to different kinds of events in your life. See whether you can identify an internal character who seems to keep occurring.

- When does this character seem to take over?
- What appears to trigger this character's appearance?
- What control do you have over this character?
- What influence does this internal character have on your leadership?
- Does this character get in the way or help?

Knowing more about these internal characters can assist you to gain leadership insight.

Courses

Workshops and training events that challenge your

existing perspective on the world and focus on how you are functioning as a person can also really help you develop greater self-awareness.

There are many different kinds of self-development courses from which to choose. Some reflect on a particular approach such as psychotherapy, psycho synthesis, transactional analysis, meditation or neuro-linguistic programming (NLP). Others are more eclectic, using a wide range of development techniques to broaden your understanding.

Give yourself a target of attending at least one self-development course every six months. See it as an enjoyable challenge, rather than a burden. After all, if you're not interested in developing you, who else will be?

In summary, growing self-awareness comes from an ongoing process of investing in your own personal development.

UNDERSTANDING OTHERS

You can apply similar methods to gain more understanding of other people. Again, it is less the method you use that is important, than your willingness to harness your natural curiosity, your determination to discover more.

With a team, for example, you might regularly ask people to explain how they are feeling, what they are thinking, what concerns them. More formally, you could ask everyone to complete a series of questionnaires that reveal their personal preferences and other information.

One of the best ways of really understanding others though, is through people-watching – consciously observing them in all kinds of different situations, observing how they behave, rather than just taking their words and actions for granted.

When you understand others you are not necessarily being clairvoyant, though that may be how it appears to less aware people. You are merely being insightful. Through intense observation, along with your other natural powers of analysis and instinct, you attempt to build up a picture of :

- Why they do what they do
- What they are feeling
- What they want
- How their words differ from their actions
- What their actions tell you
- What is *not* being said
- What it is like to be that person, rather than you

Successful leaders do not act in a vacuum. They are constantly scanning for signals to suggest what to do next. Start becoming a kind of detective, using your curiosity and interest to make sense of what is needed. Successful leaders can often mentally put themselves in their followers' shoes and guess how they will respond to different situations.

You can even do this physically. Understanding body language, for instance, concerns your ability to stand back and watch. That though, is only the first step. To really understand another person it helps to try and replicate their posture, gestures or expression. Privately imitate the person and see what it feels like to walk around and express yourself in the way that they do. You may acquire some really valuable clues about how they tick.

Best of all, ask them! It's always surprising how often this simple way of gaining a better understanding of others is neglected in favour of more elaborate and time-consuming methods. People will often tell you what they need. By not asking them, you ignore an essential source of information.

Channels

You cannot expect to always understand people by communicating through formal channels or even solely at work. You may occasionally need to sacrifice valuable personal time to socialize in non-work settings. For example, one Chief Executive who was responsible for his company's dramatic turnaround to profitability, holds a regular Monday night, five-a-side football match. People are more willing to relax and be forthcoming in social settings.

Famous leaders have often abandoned their own security or prestige surroundings in favour of hearing directly from their followers' own lips. Certain generals for instance, have even disguised themselves, so as to mingle freely with their troops and thus hear for themselves what people are thinking and saying.

The founder of WalMart in America regularly arrived at selected stores around six or seven in the morning. That way he could meet employees starting their day and spend time talking to them before they got too involved with their work.

Even when you think you have gained a clear picture of what other people are thinking, feeling or saying, you may need to check it out for accuracy. This means testing out your conclusions by asking them to say whether your view of what they think and feel is correct. Start conversations with some provocative question, for example, 'I was wondering how you felt about the current changes?' or 'You seem to be a bit quiet today, is there anything going on?'

As long as such questions are asked in an unthreatening way, you may well unearth some crucial information that will help avoid unmotivated behaviour and wasted effort.

In summary, understanding others is a continuous process of:

- Observation
- Exploration
- Testing

PERCEPTIONS OF SITUATIONS

We each view the world through our own mental maze, established over many years. No two people ever see the world identically because of our different experiences, expectations or wishes. This makes a leader's job particularly hard, since communicating to people about a situation, for instance, may challenge their unique perceptions about it.

Effective leaders see:

- Reality (theirs)
- New possibilities

Leaders see things as they really are, or differently from other people. Their reality is not always more objective or accurate, but for them it is usually more strongly held. Powerful leaders enable others to see the world through their eyes.

When an effective leader says 'this is the situation', we may not necessarily agree, yet we can respond to this interpretation, because it makes sense to us.

So, for example, the rest of us might think that newspapers are about disseminating information and news. A business leader like Rupert Murdoch though, has seen a different reality, that newspapers are more about entertainment. Those who work for him come to see this same reality.

How do leaders arrive at a different reality from the rest of us? It comes from using a different set of criteria for judging the world. This might include adopting new or discarding old:

- Views
- Prejudices
- Assumptions
- Beliefs
- Interpretations

Through their clear perception of the present situation, leaders 'see' what is needed. They do so by being alert, staying present, and so able to 're-frame' the situation until it makes sense to them and ultimately to others.

Leadership also means seeing things as they might be, in the future. If managing is organizing what already exists, then leadership is about creating possibilities and moving towards something that does not exist.

How can you improve *your* capacity to see new possibilities? Do it by expanding your creative activity in the widest sense. For example, if you value creativity you are more likely to have a significant impact on others. When leaders apply their natural creative powers to see new possibilities, later when we reflect on what they did we tend to call this form of insight, *foresight*.

To develop your foresight deliberately turn your mind towards the future by exploring:

- How can we stay ahead of the game?

- What new developments are over the horizon?
- What unexpected situations might we plan for?
- What if current trends were reversed?

'People don't recognize what they want until it is put in front of them. That's why market research is so much bunkum.'
Sir Terence Conran

Although Conran has the arrogance of somebody who has been proved right more often than wrong, there is some truth in what he says. Certainly Anita Roddick attributed much of her success to seeing which trends the cosmetic industry was following and then doing the opposite.

Looking for alternatives, seeking examples that seemingly contradict current organizational culture, noting where the rules are being broken productively, may all help your ability to see what is not yet manifest. Ask colleagues questions such as:

- What are you working on that's new or different?
- If we had a magic wand, how could we transform things around here?
- How could we make things ten times better around here?

Just as it is useful to put yourself in others' shoes and see it from their point of view, so it helps if you can stand outside a situation. Seeing it from afar often allows you to grasp the bigger picture, preventing you from becoming enmeshed in detail. This wider perspective allows you to see where things are going, or how they are developing, rather than being stuck in the current situation.

INSIGHT

Practice

Everything to do with leadership insight takes practice. Certainly some people may have been born more intuitive than others. Yet by practising observation, trying to understand other people, attempting to see reality and imagining the future you can develop your insight.

Spend some time each day just looking. Value this time as essential to the business. In these periods of reflection you may well gain an insight that could save or make your organization huge profits – far more than the day-to-day slog of repetitive activities. That's what leaders contribute.

The 7 I's
of Leadership

✦ **Taking responsibility**
✦ **Risk**
✦ **Direct action**
✦ **Vitality**

CHAPTER 2

Initiative

'I am certainly not one of those who need to be prodded. In fact if anything I am a prod.'
   Winston Churchill

Leaders are people who make things happen, who take initiative and persuade others to join their cause. You can exercise these skills anywhere, inside a company, a voluntary organization, a public agency, within a team or on the shop floor. You do not need to start your own business or command a major institution.

   Initiative really means:

   'First step; act of setting a process in motion; ability or willingness to take the lead; right or duty to make the first move; enterprise; capacity for acting independently or showing originality.'

Use initiative by taking :

* Responsibility
* Risks
* Direct action

Another clear sign that you are someone who initiates is your:

• Vitality

RESPONSIBILITY

'A *chief is a man who assumes responsibility. He says, "I was beaten"* he does not say *"my men were beaten".*'
Antoine de Saint-Exupéry

You can usually spot someone showing leadership by whether they seem ready to take responsibility. People with leadership potential put themselves forward, or they accept a role when others turn to them for help.

Look for opportunities to take responsibility through:

volunteering; participating; being accountable; taking centre stage

Volunteering – is when you keep saying 'Yes' whenever a job needs doing, or a problem needs someone to solve it. Leaders willingly take things on, often the worst jobs or the ones with least apparent kudos. The act of putting themselves forward demonstrates leadership.

For example, when you say 'Yes I'll do that' you set an example for others. You are indicating that 'this is how it should be around here'. By volunteering you model how you believe others should perform, and inspire them to take responsibility too.

Volunteering also provides opportunities to learn and grow. You open yourself to new experiences and to change. Sometimes you do not know what you are letting yourself in for. Non-leaders play it safe and avoid volunteering.

There is always the danger of overdoing it, taking on excessive work. This is destructive. Only you can judge whether you can handle more, or are heading for burn-out. Avoiding opportunities and playing safe, though, stops you having personal challenges that help realize your own potential.

Participating – another test of your leadership potential is whether you take part in other people's projects. Your willingness to join a task force, a project group, a committee, a team activity, is an important sign of leadership in an organization.

It is active not passive participation that builds leadership. Merely going along with the crowd is compliance. Active participation is demonstrating by your actions and behaviour that 'I want to contribute.'

Being accountable – shows you can be relied upon. First you make statements such as:

'I'll see that gets done'
'Leave that to me'
'That was my fault'
'I'll solve that'
'I got that wrong'
'I'll complete that on time'
'Nobody else is handling this, so I will'
'I take responsibility for that'

Secondly, you back up these promises with actions that support them.

When you act as a leader people tend to say 'She does what she says she'll do' or 'You can rely on him to do that.' By showing that you are willing to stand up and be counted you put your personal values on public display.

When a serious mistake occurs don't try to pass the buck to someone else. Instead, be willing to shoulder some or all of the blame. People will tend to see you as willing to accept criticism as well as praise. Accountability could even be taking the blame for something that is not your fault. For example, if someone responsible to you makes a serious error, as a leader you cannot hide behind them and say 'I didn't do it.' To some degree you too are in the firing line.

Unlike managers, leaders never justify what they do solely by referring to rules, company policy, job descriptions, written briefs and other ways of denying responsibility.

Taking centre stage – is another aspect of taking responsibility. You allow your leadership to be seen and acknowledged. Although some leaders can be self-effacing, ultimately all are willing to stand in the limelight of their followers' attention.

Leaders we admire tend not to place themselves at the centre; instead placing others there. They do not seek attention so much as give it to others. However, they are prepared to be in the limelight when necessary. Occasionally the limelight is more intense, when events bring you into the public eye and attract the attention of the media. Leading means being prepared to be visible in whatever form this takes. You cannot both lead and remain a shrinking violet.

RISK

It can be quite uncomfortable being a leader. In fact, what separates leaders from their supporters is a willingness to:

- Step out of their comfort zone
- Be non-compliant
- Handle rejection, disagreement and failure

Stepping out of your comfort zone – happens by attempting something unfamiliar, where you are unsure about the outcome. It is when you:

- Disagree
- Say things that may upset people
- Do things that attract disapproval
- Break the rules
- Challenge convention
- Try new things
- Do what is right, rather than what is expected
- Question received wisdom
- Act without always knowing all the likely outcomes
- Deliberately put yourself in a learning situation
- Seek information on how others see you
- Commit to action without knowing if others will follow

Your comfort zone is the area of experience where you know what to expect and how you are likely to perform. While it may be a congenial place, it is also a limiting one. It shuts you off from all sorts of experiences, feedback and situations that might help you grow and develop as a person and as a leader.

Leaving your comfort zone involves new situations where you do not know the rules or are unsure of how you will fare. Try giving yourself some systematic practice at this. For example, list twenty challenging things you would like to do, yet have never done before. These risks might be:

- **physical,** such as riding in a hot-air balloon, bungee jumping or being a blood donor
- **social,** such as attending an unusual sporting occasion, helping disabled kids, organizing a street party
- **emotional,** such as confronting somebody with a difficult truth or expressing honest feelings to a person
- **political,** such as phoning a talk-radio show, making a speech, supporting a local campaign

Or breaking a habit, or presenting yourself in an unusual way etc.

Can you think of some activities that would develop you and make you feel stretched and challenged? They may be slightly daunting or merely involve doing something you have often delayed.

Choose twelve such challenging experiences and complete one each month, for a year. By the end of it you will have had an extraordinary time, while also growing and developing in important new ways.

(Can't think of twelve such activities? Then it is time to get some fresh stimulus from talking to colleagues, going on a course, or whatever it will take to start the ball rolling.)

Yet another way of exploring your present comfort zone is to begin deliberately breaking old patterns and habits. These are not necessarily wrong, but may merely stop you seeing the world afresh, limiting your vision and no longer providing stimulus.

For example, do you always take the same route home every day? Try three different ways and notice what you learn or how it stimulates you. If you always read one type of newspaper, drink one brand of lager, get up the same time most days, experiment with doing it differently for a month. If you always tend to work late, try having a whole week in which you go home early.

List some of your more obvious patterns or habits. You may need someone else close to you to help you spot some of these. Having identified half a dozen, find ways to break them and see how you feel. If even thinking about doing so makes you uncomfortable, it could be a good reason for taking action.

Challenging your own habits and patterns makes you more open to other people, to hearing what they have to say, to learning what they want. Besides, it stops you merely going through life on auto-pilot. For example, when senior managers in supermarkets occasionally stack shelves it always gives them new perspectives.

Non-compliance – is the need to assert yourself. Being unassertive is failing to say what you think and feel, or not attempting to do what you want. By contrast leaders continuously express what they want and communicate it, until they are heard.

While sometimes it's sensible to conform, there may be more occasions when you should really listen to your own impulses to act and express yourself strongly. Do you tend to sit on these impulses, saying nothing?

Leadership is speaking your truth, even when others may strongly disagree. It is being able to say 'no' to the crowd, doing what you think is right, even if it means being different.

Generally, managers do things right or 'correctly' by following the rules. Leaders, though, take the risk of deciding for themselves what is right and do it, often regardless of any rules or the expectations of others.

When the leaders of the Boeing company launched the famous 707 airliner, it was an enormous risk that could have sunk the entire company. Conventional management thinking would almost certainly have rejected it. Yet with hindsight it was entirely the right leadership choice.

How you handle rejection, disagreement and failure is another way of taking the initiative. Few people succeed in life without some setbacks, or finding that some people disagree with them. Leaders are ready to risk the experience of people failing to support them.

Unless you ask people to do something you may never know whether they will follow your wishes. Should they refuse or fail to commit themselves wholeheartedly, you may feel abandoned, betrayed or ignored. How do leaders cope with these negative experiences?

Effective leaders never allow setbacks to dent their self-confidence or to stop them heading in the direction they want to go. Faced with setbacks they are noticeably resilient. It is often in adversity that true leadership emerges. As the ancient saying goes: any fool can steer the ship when the sea is calm.

Try exploring how you handle rejection and disagreement. When was the last time things didn't go your way? Do you allow your reactions to undermine your leadership confidence?

Fostering your own and others' self-confidence is not just about being positive. When you communicate your belief that you will succeed or that your supporters can be successful you help them to extend themselves and to persevere.

'Only he can command who has the courage and initiative to disobey.'
William McDougal, Psychologist

The best leaders keep their morale up in the face of rejection or failure by:

- Persistence
- Not personalizing
- Re-framing

Effective leaders never seem to give up, pursuing their particular vision, long after others have fallen by the wayside. *Persistence* has its own re-enforcing effect on emotions. Sheer determination can drown out the siren voices of negativity. When you are persistent despite obstacles and setbacks, you start to become inspirational.

Excessive persistence, though, can become obduracy and be unhelpful. If you keep ignoring the reality around you, blindly continuing against all the evidence, you risk rejection. Mrs Thatcher's refusal to budge over the Poll Tax for example, almost certainly helped lose her the party's leadership.

Not personalizing your setbacks is another key to dealing with rejection. Because you will face many setbacks in your leadership, it is important not to treat them as aimed at you personally. Often they are merely the result of forces beyond your immediate control. Try talking to an uninvolved person to gain a fresh perspective when your leadership seems to be meeting problems. Even leaders need mentors sometimes.

Re-framing is yet another way of dealing with setbacks and disagreements. Here you take a situation and restate it in new ways. For example, suppose you suggest that your company's computer system needs updating because it is now out of date and slow. If this proposal is rejected, rather than abandon it, you might start to re-frame the issue as a need for better communications and ways of keeping in touch with customers. From this might eventually flow a greater readiness to consider a new system.

DIRECT ACTION

'Lead, follow or get out of the way.'

Sometimes ideas become bogged down, by bureaucracy, apathy or natural resistance. No amount of talking achieves a breakthrough and something else is needed. Effective leaders recognize these situations and have a bias for action, a tendency to say 'enough talking, here's what we're going to do'.

Use your instinct and observational powers to decide when to stop the talking and start the action.

To get things moving leaders willingly risk criticism, reprimands or worse. For example, the Hollywood producer Dawn Steel, later Paramount's production director, was passionate about making the film *Flashdance*, which later became a huge international success. After overcoming many setbacks she realized that a major obstacle was her own boss. She took him out to lunch and announced she was leaving 'because if you won't back me on this film, you're never going to back me on anything else'. He changed his mind and supported her project.

Direct action means making something happen, sometimes regardless of whether this has immediate benefits. Often the decision provides the essential leverage to move forward. Leaders realize that there are occasions when a decision – any decision – is better than none at all.

VITALITY

Meet any effective leader and you are almost always struck by their vitality. This is only partly a gift of the gods. It is also a result of using their energy to stay wide awake, be constantly alert and naturally curious.

Vitality is hard to define precisely although, like leadership itself, you certainly know it when you see it.

'I think enthusiasm rubs off on people, like pollen on bees.'
Sir Terence Conran

You cannot expect to have vitality unless you are healthy, which means paying attention to the needs of your

- Body
- Mind
- Spirit

Busy people often neglect exercise, without realizing its contribution to their leadership potential. Regular exercise does more than keep in trim your muscles and other organs. It's like air-conditioning for the brain. It blows away the mental cobwebs and contributes to your state of alertness.

Managers often pay lip-service to maintaining a balance between work and non-work. Effective leaders, though, know it's essential for retaining their natural vitality. Richard Branson's balloon escapades may have had publicity gains; less obviously they helped him to maintain and enhance his enjoyment of life and hence his natural vitality.

Leisure and holidays are essential for sustaining leadership energy. It is all too easy to burn out from work. The very word recreation is about re-creating your vitality. The best leaders realize that they need to take care of themselves to minimize the impact of stress.

Work often expresses who we are. Leaders create the work they want, rather than react to what is thrown at them. Being aware of the bigger picture of one's life is another powerful way of staying sane.

'One of the symptoms of an approaching nervous breakdown is the belief that one's work is terribly important.'
Bertrand Russell

Vitality also stems from being open to *personal growth and learning*. To realize your full potential as a leader means discovering as much about yourself as possible, both your strengths and your own development needs.

Gaining the support of others is another important source of vitality. People love to be asked for their help. You can only create supporters by making room for people's contribution.

Being willing to say 'I don't know', is also a sign of strength, rather than weakness, as long as it's not a constant theme in your conversations. Allow yourself to be nurtured by others around you. To lead you do not need to be omnipotent.

The 7 I's of Leadership

✦ **Vision**
✦ **Communication**
✦ **Passion**
✦ **Trust**

CHAPTER 3

Inspiration

Leaders inspire, managers motivate. It is perfectly possible to survive as a manager without ever inspiring anyone. However you cannot be a leader without an ability to inspire.

What is inspiration? In essence it's a feeling, an experience. We are moved in some way. Its result is that people feel different and are willing to do unusual things: go beyond their present limits, show courage, deal with formidable odds, cope with impossible circumstances.

Often the most basic experiences can be unbelievably inspiring, such as a daily sunset or the birth of a child. In business, inspiration usually emerges as enabling people to perform beyond their normal limits, to go that extra mile, produce outstanding results and look forward to coming to work.

'And then there is inspiration. Where does it come from? Mostly from the excitement of living. I get it from the diversity of a tree or the ripple of the sea, a bit of poetry, the sighting of a dolphin breaking the still water and moving toward me ... anything that quickens you to the instant.'

Martha Graham, dancer and teacher

Managers tend to see motivation as something *done* to people. True leaders, though, are more concerned with: awakening, stimulus, spirit, energy, zeal, enthusiasm, vigour, gusto, ebullience, sparkle. These are what make people support a leader.

Traditionally we associate inspiration as the preserve of artists or charismatic personalities. Yet when anyone has a good idea or feels strongly about something they can be inspiring to other people. When someone is inspired it is as if they have received a spark of genius from some other world. Such moments may appear to be totally fortuitous, but often they come as a result of a period of intense work.

'Inspiration is a guest who doesn't like to visit lazy people.'
Tchaikovsky

Although Tchaikovsky implies that it is hard work that leads to inspiration we suggest that how you work is equally important. Working smarter not harder may be the way to gain inspiration.

You can learn to inspire other people, not once but often. The inescapable starting point is:

To inspire others, first inspire yourself

Discovering what inspires you is always the first step to having an effect on other people. Making this discovery means you need to:

- Immerse yourself in what seems to get you excited, moves you, makes you feel uplifted
- Be willing to explore what inspires others
- Start making a list of events, poems, works of art,

films, books, people, plays, scenery or whatever, that
inspires you
- Start distinguishing between the mediocre and the
inspirational

Leaders work hard at inspiration and know that it
doesn't always come easy. Make a choice to spend as
much time as you can with whatever it is that, for you,
rises above the mundane.

When you are inspired you are passionate, persuasive, unselfconscious and a great communicator. Everyone has that potential, leaders just do it more often.
Although one cannot reduce it to a simple formula the
commonest elements are:

- Vision
- Communication
- Passion
- Trust

VISION

*'The single defining quality of leaders is the capacity to
create and realize a vision.'*
Warren Bennis, US leadership expert

All leaders create a compelling vision, one that promises
to take their supporters to a new place. Then they show
how to turn that vision into a reality. You do not need
to be unusually prescient, it is more to do with defining
what you want the future to look like.

President George Bush complained he lacked 'the
vision thing', while the newly appointed head of IBM
whose job was to rescue the ailing giant said 'the last

thing IBM needs is a vision'. Both failed to realize that vision was not a vague dream of the future, but an intensely clear idea of what they wanted the future to look like.

Sometimes we resist working with vision because we think it is the privilege of only gifted people. However, if you have ever walked into a run-down flat or house and had an idea of how it could look, you are in the realm of vision. Being able to imagine it decorated and furnished is a good start.

Similarly you create a picture for yourself of how your office could ideally function, or your team might perform brilliantly together, or your organization thrive.

'I dream for a living.'
Steven Spielberg

Where does vision come from? It would be wonderful to wake one morning with a compelling one and doubtless some exceptional leaders do work that way. However, more often it requires a struggle to articulate vision, and you may need help from your supporters to:

- identify the vision
- expand the vision
- translate it into a message that everyone can understand

For example, Federal Express's famous three-word vision is *'People, Service, Profit'*. Yet this apparently simple three-word picture of what drives the company took a considerable time to evolve.

Vision operates in companies on three distinct levels:

- Strategic
- Tactical
- Personal

Strategic vision is the organization's overriding philosophy and provides the framework into which all activities fit. Somebody has to hold this vision, never losing sight of it. This might be the chief executive or the top management team. Ideally it is owned by everyone. For example, the strategic vision of Komatsu was to 'Beat Caterpillar', the then market leader for tractors and heavy earth-moving vehicles. Everybody in Komatsu knew and understood what this strategic vision meant.

Tactical vision is the philosophy in action and provides people with clear methods for taking action. Often tactical vision comes down to a picture of how the strategic vision will be achieved. For example, 'To value quality above all else.'

Personal vision exists when each person in their own unique way starts behaving so as to realize the vision. For example, a chalk board in one company's head office shows a list of personal commitments by managers that they believe will contribute to the company's strategic vision.

A strategic vision in business is not enough. As a leader you will need to be concerned with both the tactical and personal aspects. For example, effective leaders want to know how their colleagues are understanding and interpreting the vision, 'on the ground'.

A prevalent myth is that vision is always the invention of a single leader. It is more frequently the result of groups of people working in harmony towards a common aim. Arriving at the common aim may be difficult as people strive to create a joint picture of the future that inspires them. The leadership role is simply to oil the wheels of this creative process.

Another way of tapping into your own or your team's vision, is to explore your own values. These are your core beliefs that you do not easily alter. You can begin to determine them by answering the question:

'What really matters to me is . . .'

What *does* matter to you? Is it waste, injustice, poverty, happiness, love, winning, or what? Try making a list of the five most important values in your life. Use these to help you begin building a picture of your vision of the future you want to create.

Many managers who are potential leaders fail through their impatience with the whole concept of vision. Because it is conceptual, they don't take the time to develop and refine it. Those who are most action-minded tend to reject it as 'airy-fairy stuff' or insufficiently connected with the real world.

Yet there is nothing more real than a compelling vision. People 'see' what could be, and are prepared to do extraordinary things to realize it.

'When a vision begins to form everything changes, including the air around me.'
Jean Dixon in Ruth Montgomery, *A Gift of Prophesy*

COMMUNICATION

A vision that stays locked inside your head is useless. If you really care about your vision you will *want* to share it with others. It will inspire and excite you to the point where you cannot help telling other people about it.

Most effective managers are good communicators and leaders are even better at it. You do not need to persuade a leader that presentation matters, or that their message needs to have impact. They are already convinced. You may well need to refine your communication skills if you are to lead successfully. You can do this in several ways:

- Think visually
- Use specific, practical examples
- Keep your messages short
- Explain the likely results of what you want
- Show personal commitment
- Ceaselessly talk about your vision to others
- Listen carefully
- Practise new ways of explaining your leadership message

Thinking visually means developing ways of conveying your vision to build pictures in people's minds. Strive to create an image of what you want, an almost tangible visualization of how the future should look. This requires practice. Start by thinking of images that already strike you as powerful, whether these are advertising pictures, paintings, a scene from a film or a photograph from a book.

Using images gives practice to the part of the brain that works by instinct, feeling and non-verbal concepts. You can also use metaphors as ideas that convey what you want. For example, by imagining your growing company as yeast fermenting you are using a metaphor to express a vision.

What image would summarize the future you want to create? Finding a powerful image or interesting metaphor to describe it helps other people 'see' what you are seeking. Martin Luther King's famous 'I have a dream' speech is a perfect example of using image to encapsulate a vision.

Use specific, practical examples to bring your vision to life. People understand messages best through real instances to which they can personally relate. For instance, by telling people how they will be affected by what you want to do, you are starting to turn vision into a reality.

Keep your messages short to avoid clogging the communication channels. This is not the same as being a speaker of few words. Effective leaders realize that at any one moment people can only absorb a certain amount of information, and they become expert at reducing their communications to extremely simple ideas.

Explain the likely results of what you want. People need to understand how they will be affected by what you want to achieve. Use examples to bring these results to life. Suppose a company's vision is that it should be the customer's first choice, this might start to be translated into practical tasks such as always ensuring that the phone is answered within three rings.

Show personal commitment to what you want to achieve. This can be summed up as sharing your feelings with supporters. If you do not care, why should they? (See below, Passion.) Model the required behaviour. For example, if you wish to sponsor excellent customer care, then start by caring for your staff in an exceptional way.

Ceaselessly talk about your vision to others. Leaders persistently talk about what they want, what matters, what the vision is all about. To get your message across requires constant communication. This does not mean being a loud-mouthed bore. Just keep watching for any opportunity to share your ideals.

Listen carefully to what others have to say about your vision. This will help you to refine it. Communication is two-way and merely banging on about your idea stops you receiving some invaluable input. Let people play devil's advocate with your idea. It will help you to clarify it and make you even more able to communicate it effectively.

PASSION

Call it passion, commitment or conviction. Whatever the name, powerful leaders have it in large measure. They also insist on sharing it, constantly. Their passion is not directionless. It is sharply focused around what they want to achieve. It is concentrated and, like a laser beam, cuts through objections, obstacles and negativity. It is hard to say no to someone who cares so strongly about something and difficult to resist being drawn into their vision and becoming engaged.

In business it is now more acceptable to talk of commitment or conviction than a decade ago. Effective leaders soon learn that it is passion that moves people to support them, not appeals to logic or a recital of facts and figures.

For anyone wanting to be an effective leader the good news is that when you have found your passion you have a technique of immense power. The bad news is that you have to really care, it cannot be faked. People somehow know when your passion is forced.

As a leadership tool passion is commonly misunderstood as meaning a ranting, excessively emotional appeal that sets many people's teeth on edge. In politicians this becomes demagoguery.

The passion that truly works is when you are emotionally connected to what you want to happen. When you make that connection you sound convincing and others find their emotions engaged too.

Start by listing your passions. Many of us run away from strong emotions and then wonder why others find us boring or unconvincing. When you use your passion you are also vulnerable since you are sharing with others what really matters to you. If they reject what you want, in some sense they seem to be rejecting you too.

Passionate leaders are unafraid to let their feelings come through. You can only expect to move others if you are willing to be moved yourself. This does not necessarily mean you are reduced to a tearful mess, though more than one leader has allowed tears to flow in the passion of the moment.

Passion in leadership is about first becoming absolutely convinced of the importance of what you want to happen and then being totally willing to share that strong feeling with others.

TRUST

To inspire people to participate, they need to trust both you and themselves. To engender trust you:

- Trust yourself
- Do what you say you will do
- Are reliable
- Trust others

When you trust yourself, you are willing to:

- Listen to that inner voice
- Use your natural instincts

- Allow feelings to play an important, though not necessarily always dominant part in guiding your actions

'The only way to make a man trustworthy is to trust him.'
    Henry Stimson, US Secretary of War 1990

The perfect leader builds trust slowly, starting small. For example, you create trust in others when you always do what you say you will do – because effective leaders honour their word. They are consistent in their approach and their policy. Thus leaders partly attract people because they can be relied upon. When you are reliable, people will naturally tend to ask your opinions, seek your help, follow your guidance.

Having developed trust in yourself and shown you trust others, you are ready to move on to helping people learn to trust each other. If you lead a team, for example, this is a crucial part of your job. There may be many creative ways you can discover to engender this trust, some of which may work more quickly than others.

For example, taking your team away for one or two days to focus on how you all work together builds trust. It creates it both between individual team members, and ultimately between the team and the leader. You are unlikely to allow such an investment in team time if you do not first of all trust yourself, and your contribution to the team.

'Trust your hopes, not your fears.'
    David Mahoney, chairman, Norton Simon Inc.

Managers who complain that they find it hard to gain people's trust are usually those who have little real faith in themselves and what they want to do. Instead they rely on authority and the power of position to obtain what they want. The trouble is that this way of working is rapidly becoming obsolete.

When you trust other people to perform better than they think they can, you are certainly taking a gamble. It is the kind of gamble, though, that effective leaders take constantly. They rely on others performing beyond their normal limitations, it's how they inspire them, through sharing their expectation that their supporters will do extraordinary things.

Where mutual trust does not exist, people are cautious, less open, less influential, more distant and more inclined to leave at the first opportunity. True leadership is getting ordinary people to do extraordinary things. That's inspirational.

The 7 I's
of Leadership

+ **Enrolment**
+ **Empowerment**
+ **Personal investment**
+ **Feedback**
+ **Stakeholders**

CHAPTER 4

Involvement

Managers devolve, leaders involve. It takes real leadership for people to feel genuinely part of the vision and fully committed to realizing it. Too often, lip-service is paid to the idea of involving people.

There are various ways to begin involving people in what you want to achieve:

- Enrolment
- Empowerment
- Personal investment
- Feedback
- Identifying stakeholders

ENROLMENT

In the days of navy press gangs, one trick was to slip a coin into someone's drink. Once the unfortunate person had downed his beer, he had unwittingly 'accepted the King's shilling' and was now legally employed by His Majesty's Navy. Press-ganged people, though, made poor sailors. At the first chance many deserted, so the process had to start all over again.

Trying to force someone's enrolment is like shouting 'grow' at a plant. While it may sound impressive it is unlikely to achieve much. Effective enrolment occurs when someone 'buys into' what you want to achieve. That is, they take the important step of saying 'yes I'd like to be part of that'. In effect they are 'signing on'.

People only 'buy in' or 'sign on' under certain circumstances. To achieve that means discovering how to engage their interest, awaken their curiosity, tap their ambition, challenge them, arouse enthusiasm, deal with their fears and so on.

When someone enrols, he or she becomes committed to following your lead. This starts with learning what you want to achieve, feeling potentially part of the grand design, understanding one's possible role. To achieve these:

- Communicate your purpose
- Ask people to join you in working towards the goal
- Say why you need their help
- Describe how they personally can affect the outcome
- Invite them to declare what they need to feel enrolled
- Describe how the end result will affect them personally
- Explain the likely consequences of not enrolling

All these rely on you being a powerful presenter of your purpose. Only if people really begin to 'see' and understand it can they make up their minds to 'buy in'. All effective leaders are powerful presenters, so if this is your weak area, consider investing in some further training.

Apart from putting your message across well, encourage enrolment through directly asking people if they will join with you in the purpose. You are not asking their permission, just checking that they are with you.

Potential supporters also need to know *why* you require their help. This is not simply about requiring their particular skills. It means wanting them for who they are. Naturally this demands sufficient contact with them to explain just why you believe they are vital to the purpose.

As you enrol people in your projects and they realize the difference their contribution can make, so they can create their own support. Encourage people to do this and you create a spiral of involvement that will strengthen your effectiveness.

If you are head of a large organization, or department, making contact with everyone is extremely difficult. You are less convincing at a distance, so it always pays to try and do this face to face with people. Videos, memos, e-mail and other such devices are no substitute for people meeting you personally to hear about the purpose and learning how much you care about it.

Often, though, you will have to rely on others to do the contacting for you. This is why your selection of those closest to you is so crucial.

Invite people to say what they require to feel enrolled. It might be anything from a hefty salary to a challenging new role. You can seldom take people's enrolment for granted, even if they have agreed to be employed by you. Try and uncover what they themselves feel would make them committed to the purpose.

Potential supporters want to know 'How will I be affected if I join in?' They may take a great deal on trust. Yet the more you can explain how the end result will affect them, the more you make it easy for them to take that vital first step.

Spell out clearly any adverse consequences of not

enrolling, such as losing out on important benefits. Avoid making this information into a direct threat. Also, if you do paint a thoroughly negative picture of the adverse consequences be sure it has credibility.

A powerful way leaders obtain enrolment is by enabling people to realize they will be engaged in achieving something extraordinary. How can you expect them to enrol if what is on offer is pedestrian? It must capture their imagination, making them feel that whatever they will be travelling towards is a worthwhile destination.

Effective leaders develop the knack of explaining how even the simplest tasks link to the grand design.

EMPOWERMENT

'When the best leaders' work is done, the people say: "We did it ourselves."'
Lau-Tzu

Leadership by just issuing orders and attempting to control everything has never really worked well in business organizations, for long. Into the next century leadership is about sharing power, giving support to others so they feel inspired to do great things.

In simple terms, empowerment means giving people responsibility, the right to make decisions and take more charge of their lives.

When people have the autonomy to take over all aspects of management, including work, holiday scheduling, ordering materials, and hiring new team members, the results are nearly always spectacular gains in productivity and creativity.

Paradoxically, by releasing some of your leadership authority you actually enhance it. People then feel more able to ask for your help, to hear your suggestions and to follow your lead. Some of the known results include:

- revitalized employees
- increased morale
- increased productivity
- improved quality
- lower staff turnover

There are innumerable ways to empower through your leadership. Just be creative in discovering which ones work best for you and your supporters. Successful approaches include to:

- Show people they are not separate from management and that they can help the organization improve
- Demonstrate that good ideas are implemented
- Appreciate and reward suggestions even if they are not implemented
- Trust people with responsibility
- Respect people's ideas and judgement
- Allow people to make decisions

PERSONAL INVESTMENT

Enrolment and empowerment are easier to achieve when people have a personal investment in the vision or purpose. This is not necessarily financial investment. It is putting some important aspects of themselves into the work, such as:

- Time
- Energy
- Creativity

- Ideas
- Know-how
- Personal resources such as information and contacts
- Personal development
- Formal training
- Creating important relationships

Check on the personal investment your supporters are making. People who have made a personal investment are less likely to fall away when the going gets rough.

Financially rewarding people who give their commitment and involvement also makes good sense. Companies like Land Rover, for example, offer substantial financial incentives for suggestions from individuals. They also offer rewards to teams of employees who have made a collective recommendation. Thus people see tangible evidence that involvement pays.

Encourage through modelling your own personal investment.

When you demonstrate that you too have a major personal investment in the vision or purpose, others are more likely to follow. When you enlist people's personal investment you do not need to motivate them, they are already motivated.

FEEDBACK

Actors rehearse and receive continual information about their performance from both their director and ultimately the audience. Musicians look to the conductor both during rehearsals and in the actual performance for guidance on how they are doing.

Leaders are no different. They too need continual feedback on how they are doing and the best ones keep seeking out this information from innumerable channels, both formal and informal.

Feedback is how people influence a leader's plans and contribute to the vision. If you try doing this without this essential information you risk being on the receiving end of some nasty, and for your leadership perhaps fatal, surprises.

Ensure that your own performance is continually monitored.

Hearing others' opinions is an invaluable resource and the best leaders are hungry to hear what people have to say.

IDENTIFYING STAKEHOLDERS

Which people? To whom should a leader listen so as to monitor personal performance and learn what supporters want? There are probably many different sorts of people with a stake in your success – the stakeholders.

Make a list of those who either benefit, or are involved in some way with what you want to achieve. For instance, if you are the leader of a board of school governors, the children, parents, teachers, administrators, unions, governors, council, inspectors and perhaps others are all part of the well-being of the school.

For a leader in a company the list includes staff, customers, directors, shareholders, as well as perhaps local residents, unions, professional associations, and even charities or community groups who benefit from the company's success. For example, many community groups would be adversely affected if The Body Shop and its leaders began to fail, since the company is deeply involved in supporting local projects.

All such groups may have a part to play in your plans, in helping to realize your vision. The more you actively involve them, the more energy you have available to get the job done.

People become involved when they feel they can affect the outcome. So the sooner you begin to involve your stakeholders in supporting your ideas and intentions the better. Rather than having to struggle to convince people when you are well along the road towards your vision, they can learn as they go.

Leadership is about a relationship with the stakeholders, creating a working partnership. The clearer and more powerful your picture of what you want to achieve, the more likely you are to be able to draw stakeholders in to support you.

It can be both surprising and satisfying to discover that your stakeholders have some strong views on how to help you succeed as a leader. WalMart's founder relied heavily on getting everyone to tell him what he needed to do to develop his organization, even though he had plenty of his own ideas.

'Too bad that all the people who know how to run the country are busy driving taxicabs and cutting hair.'
George Burns

Blocks
Naturally there are obstacles to involving people fully. Some of these belong to you, and some to them. Let's start with your own.

A prison governor once declared, 'This would be a great place if only we didn't have to fill it with criminals.' For some companies, everything would be fine if only they didn't have to bother with customers. Leaders could say much the same: 'I could be a great leader if only I didn't need supporters.'

It's nearly always a headache dealing with other people and their wants. For leaders and managers it usually feels easier to do many things oneself. That way you don't have to worry about allowing for other people's views and their apparent limitations. It usually takes more time and energy initially to teach somebody else to do a job that you know you can do quicker and better yourself.

As a leader you may need to work hard at resisting your natural temptation to keep doing things yourself, and bypassing your supporters. One of the commonest blocks to being an effective leader is being a control freak – wanting to somehow keep a grip on everything.

The best leaders learn to let go. They continually hand over relevant power and responsibility to others. However, they always retain the right to know what is going on.

Another block is your own reactions to hearing what your supporters have to say. Because you know the broader picture, it is all too easy to be resentful or over-confident that you know best.

If you are really going to listen to stakeholders and others then you may not be able to have everything your own way. That is the price for working collaboratively.

Other people
If you encourage people to be part of your vision, enrol them and obtain their commitment, they may also want some of your power. Otherwise why should they become so involved?

You will almost certainly need to overcome people's

natural inertia or apathy, their cynicism, distrust, or resistance. However, this is all part of leading. Your refusal to be dragged down by such negative forces is partly what sets you apart from others.

The difficulties you will face with supporters is part of the job. Leadership is seldom plain sailing and dealing with obstacles, your own and other people's, is what allows you to personally grow and develop.

IN SUMMARY

Leaders only achieve their dreams through others. When approaching any project, it is worth asking yourself:

- Who else could be involved?
- What specific support can they give me?
- What will they need to be involved (what's in it for them)?
- How can I involve them?

By answering these questions and devising a way of addressing each one, you stand a far better chance of attaining your vision.

The 7 I's of Leadership

+ **Creativity**
+ **Flexibility**
+ **Presence**

CHAPTER 5

Improvisation

In one of the Indiana Jones films, when the hero is asked about his plan for getting out of trouble, he admits, 'I don't know, I'm just making it up as I go along.' That is why many business leaders are effective too, and why what they do so often differs from more conventional management.

Because something worked last time, it is no guarantee that it will work again. Like Indiana Jones you need to be willing to invent it as you go along.

There are no cast-iron rules of leading. Even if there were, they would certainly alter once you began relying on them. Instead, expand your ability to improvise, to think on your feet, to be creative in any moment, and respond to what is around you. That way you too can do it like it has never been done before. This is how you lead people in a rapidly changing world.

Doing it like it has never been done before is one of the most important aspects of business leadership. When the creator of Federal Express, for example, based the delivery company on a wheel-and-spoke principle, there were many in the industry who had already known and dismissed the concept. Yet none had possessed the courage to put it into effect.

Similarly, the idea of instant and continuous news had been around for years when Ted Turner launched CNN. Many people, in fact, predicted that it would lose a fortune. It took genuine leadership to press ahead regardless, doing what no one else had done so far.

When leaders improvise they use:

- Creativity
- Flexibility
- Presence

CREATIVITY

'Resist the usual.'
Raymond Rubicam

We usually think of creativity in simple terms such as being an artist, or perhaps generating lists of new ideas. In fact, leadership creativity is much wider and includes many different aspects of doing things differently. It requires you to:

- Innovate
- Stimulate others
- Create a 'try it' environment
- Problem-solve
- Receive and reward others' ideas

Innovation
'Every act of creation is first of all an act of destruction.'
Pablo Picasso

Creativity in leadership is not necessarily being innovative yourself, though that certainly helps. It is even more important that you enable others to innovate on your behalf. It ought to be in every business leader's job description that they are personally responsible for ensuring the organization actively encourages innovation, in its many manifestations.

Innovation often means making something from nothing. Leaders take limited resources and weld them into new combinations, so that something original or different can occur. In business, this mainly happens through identifying key issues and creating powerful teams, project groups, alliances and networks.

The leadership impulse to innovate stems from the drive to initiate – one of the 7 I's of leadership. Doing it successfully depends partly on your own creative process so explore what makes you creative through discovering:

- How do I best tap my natural creativity?
- What triggers my creativity?
- When do I get my ideas?
- How do I usually respond to other people's creativity?
- How often do I take regular time for reflection?

The last of these is much underrated. Standing back and thinking, giving yourself time and space to ruminate and allowing thoughts to wander is not wasted idleness. We need such times. For busy leaders it is particularly hard to obtain them and important that they do.

You can spend weeks or months struggling to force out cost-cutting ideas to save your company money. With time to reflect, you might help produce the answer in ten minutes. By understanding and valuing your own creative process you strengthen your leadership capability.

'A significant number of big money ideas have occurred to me whilst on vacation.'

Nolan Bushnell, entrepreneur/inventor, founder of Atari

Stimulate others

Leadership creativity also stems from enabling others to be inventive and original. Study how to trigger creativity in individuals and teams. Everyone can do it, they may just need a stimulus. Leaders provide the stimulus.

Discovering what triggers a team's creativity, for example, gives you a powerful tool for making things happen. It is therefore worth learning what works and what does not. Also, people need time to practise being creative, to discover for themselves how best they can do it. Use team meetings to explore creating together. Whether it is brain-storming to tackle a problem, or other creative techniques, every meeting can be a laboratory of invention.

You can set people problems, rotate the chairing role, ask team members to prepare papers and ideas on a subject, suggest they bring in examples of creative work from outside the business – anything to get them buzzing and experimenting.

Your leadership contribution is to provide relevant challenges that stimulate people to find new resources within themselves to create. Even if you genuinely believe they can do this, it is not enough by itself. Communicate it, showing clearly that you have faith in their innate ability to achieve breakthroughs.

A 'try it' environment

At the heart of creativity lies the freedom to experiment and make mistakes. It is a hard freedom for some organizations to tolerate. The drive for fault-free, quality actions may conflict with the right to make mistakes and learn from them.

An important contribution you can make is demonstrating that you want to learn what works through experimentation. By 'modelling' such behaviour you will help others to see the importance of it.

Practise giving a 'let's try it and see' response, when people produce ideas. This is much preferable to 'Yes but' or 'But' in response to suggestions. People soon learn from your example. When you show that it is all right to experiment, they will tend to convey the same message to others with whom they work.

Underpinning the freedom to experiment are:

- Clarifying the learning
- Not punishing people for mistakes
- Underlining that the only unacceptable mistakes are ones that could 'hole the ship below the waterline'

When you focus on 'what can we learn from this mistake?' rather than 'who's to blame?', you ensure that lessons are not lost for the future. This helps to make your company a 'learning organization'. Cherish mistakes as invaluable opportunities for learning.

'If I had to live my life again, I'd make the same mistakes, only sooner.'
Tallulah Bankhead

Punishing people for mistakes is a great way to kill off ideas. Once people realize they will suffer retribution when things go awry, they soon learn to play it safe. This is fine if you see an organization merely as a machine, with the people in it merely cogs. However, this approach is almost certainly bound to fail in our fast-moving world where it is often more important to be flexible than to always get things right.

The freedom to make mistakes is not a licence to be reckless. You do not ignore mistakes by simply shrugging your shoulders and saying 'that's too bad'. Rather, you use them as an opportunity to encourage yet more learning, to get it right next time, to build fail-safe systems.

'An executive who had lost £10 million at IBM was called to meet Thomas Watson Jr, president of the company. "Do you know why you are here?" he asked. "I suppose you're going to fire me?" the anxious executive replied. "Fire you! Are you crazy? I've just spent £10 million on your education."'

Try adopting the principle that people can make mistakes but are not permitted to 'hole the ship below the waterline'. This has stood the test of time. The failure to use it and build sufficient control systems, enabled the maverick dealer Leeson in Singapore to destroy the Barings banking group.

The more you personally commit to the idea of experimentation the better. Involve your team, customers and other stakeholders in your experiments so that they are all sharing the success and any possible failure.

Offer hypotheses for people in the organization to test. For example, you might suggest that there is a growing market for a new type of service. Presenting this as a hypothesis for testing makes it more likely that you will uncover the truth, rather than having your supporters merely trying to prove you right.

Problem solving

Most work is about solving problems in some form. The more interesting the problem, the more absorbing the work. Most problems are solved easily in the everyday activity of work, using information gained while solving previous problems. Occasionally though, problems arise that are tricky and these are the ones that leaders usually face. Such problems normally have few precedents, requiring a creative response.

We so often spend considerable time worrying about what isn't working rather than putting our attention on what a solution might look like. Imagine how things could be if the problem was overcome. Draw it as a picture or as a symbol. This may help you gain access to the right-hand side of your brain that does not think logically but thinks visually and holistically.

Brain-storming, in which you produce lots of ideas without initially criticizing or rejecting them, can start your natural, subconscious creative powers working. So, involve others and practise 'playing' with the problem. A sense of fun and a lighthearted approach can often release unforeseen solutions for even the most serious difficulties.

Focus on solutions, not obstacles

Receive and reward others' ideas

Companies and teams are full of good ideas, though half of them never get beyond their office doors. As a leader it's your responsibility to find ways of communicating that swiftly move any new idea from source to where it's needed. Suggestion boxes, e-mail systems, open communication – every opportunity can be used to process good ideas so that they can be used quickly.

Many companies have remuneration systems, not

just for individuals who have ideas, but for teams throughout the organization. These can be linked to the profit they create for the organization. You can create a culture that rewards innovation so that money is used to generate new ideas. However, money is not the only important factor. Equally important is how new ideas are received by you and other people. A 'yes' culture responds to new ideas with an open mind: 'yes, we might try that'. Only after this initial response does the more cautious aspect of screening the idea really start.

FLEXIBILITY

'It is an old ironic habit of human beings, to run faster when we have lost our way.'
   Rollo May

People have a habit of persistently pursuing actions even when they are patently not getting anywhere. The first rule of holes is: if you're in one, stop digging.

   Improvisation is about flexibility. Being able to adjust and adapt to situations is one of our prime abilities as human beings. Flexible thinking lets us resist primitive impulses to carry on regardless of the evidence.

   Water is a great symbol of flexible power. If it cannot follow a direct course, it will always find a way through, winding around and adapting to the terrain. Yet its power will always move it onwards.

Clarity
The clearer your vision, purpose or objective, the easier it becomes to be flexible in how you achieve it. Not only

may there be many routes to your destination, you may even invent ones that never before existed. By always focusing on the end result, you retain the larger picture. Leaders hold the picture as their guiding star.

'If I don't get there headed straight, maybe I get there by zigzagging, or jumping over the problem.'
Dr. Nathan Kline, psychiatrist and researcher

Openness
Being open to people's ideas can supply you with more choices, some of which may be better than others. Releasing control generates other possibilities. Improvisation creates new solutions. Go with the flow of events, rather than always pushing against them.

When a leader shows flexibility this helps avoid a frenzied reaction to any obstacle, and promotes a creative response. Responding means taking responsibility for using new information and putting it to work.

To respond productively so that you can improvise, you also need to be alert and present.

PRESENCE

'Talking to him I felt I was the most important person in the room at that moment.' Great leaders have the knack of giving you their full attention, at least for a while. They seem to be utterly present, seeing what's happening in the moment.

We are daily bombarded by millions of pieces of information. To prioritize and filter the data you need to be receptive to it. So often people simply miss what's going on around them – the very stimulus needed to get one's creativity going.

Many leaders talk about every minute being an opportunity to move the business on, to transform the situation, to create something out of nothing. This implies an intense awareness of moment to moment, a sense of staying conscious to how life changes continuously.

Leaders develop a heightened awareness of those moments of life and how quickly they disappear. This means being sensitive, as we described in Chapter 1, and also using your senses, particularly:

- **Seeing.** Look around at what's happening now; be alert to what's going on; are there opportunities staring you in the face right now?
- **Listening.** We are sometimes so busy planning what we're going to say that we don't listen. True listening is active, not a passive way of waiting for your turn to speak.

  Notice how often you are listening to the voice in your head, rather than fully absorbing what is being said to you. Leaders listen with respect and purpose. They are always asking 'what can I hear that will move us forward and how can I contribute to it?'

  Impressive listening skills have been shown to be one of the common characteristics of credible leaders.
- **Feeling.** Work at becoming more aware of your feelings. These are clues to what excites you and others. Feelings help define: the best decisions, what actions will inspire people, what's going on that others will want to be part of.

SUMMARY

No matter how well we plan, the unforeseen will always threaten our strategy. By actively developing your ability to improvise, you mobilize a whole armoury of new resources to help realize your vision.

The 7 I's of Leadership

- ✦ Being yourself
- ✦ Personal experience
- ✦ Style
- ✦ Values
- ✦ Integrity
- ✦ Networking

CHAPTER 6

Individuality

'We boil at different degrees,' wrote Emerson, neatly capturing our mutual individuality. Leaders are unafraid of being different, in most cases revelling in it. Being different is a gift each of us possesses, though not everyone cherishes it the way effective leaders do.

Paradoxically the best leaders convince people that they are one of them, yet also exceptional. Almost by definition, a leader stands out from others, if only by taking the lead. Leadership individuality stems from:

- Being yourself
- Using personal experience
- Style
- Personal values
- Integrity
- Building networks

BEING YOURSELF

It is hard to be yourself when all around there are pressures to make you into someone else. Pressure from the media, your friends, and the organization, may all conspire to suggest that who you are is less important than what you do. Yet who you are really matters, it is one of the crucial elements underpinning true leadership.

To be truly yourself is to possess considerable self-knowledge, which does not just 'happen'. It occurs because you:

- Are your own best teacher
- Accept responsibilities without blaming others
- Realize that you can learn anything you want to learn
- Reflect on your experiences

It can be summed up as:

- Being true to yourself
- Accepting yourself with all your strengths and weaknesses

When you accept who you are, you admire other people without trying to be them. Because Richard Branson, for example, walks round in sweaters and casual trousers does not mean everyone who leads a successful business should do the same. Anita Roddick of The Body Shop is notorious for a rather flyaway hairstyle, which is no reason for other leaders in the cosmetics industry to copy her.

Two further aspects of being yourself are:

- Being distinctive
- Personal identity

Being distinctive
It is strange that the more you are yourself, the more distinctive you appear to others. Uniqueness speaks for

itself, helping you stand out from the crowd. There is no universal formula for being distinctive. Each leader does it differently.

Describing one of Charlemagne's chiefs, someone observed: 'Nature made him and then broke the mould.' How followers and others talk about a leader usually amounts to saying this person is really 'one of a kind'.

Are you prepared to value your distinctiveness? You could be distinctive by how you walk, talk, deal with people, get things done, dress, communicate, define or solve problems, follow your convictions and so on. For example, are you proud of your regional accent or do you try to hide it? Do you love bold colours, yet avoid wearing them because certain people might not approve? If you really believe in something do you say so, or conceal it?

Similarly, when you meet resistance, is your reaction to slow down or back track? Will you risk becoming a target for people jealous of your difference, of your determination to achieve results? Others may not want you to stand out, or be antagonized by your refusal to be anonymous. Such is the price of leadership. Are you willing to pay it?

'The thing that makes you exceptional is inevitably that which must also make you lonely.'
Lorraine Hansberry, *Young, Gifted and Black*

Personal identity
Effective leaders possess a clear sense of their personal identity, linked to what they want – their destiny. Who they are defines what they want to achieve.

A clear sense of who you are lets you take risks, and step out. Believing that whatever you do never funda-mentally alters your essential self means you are secure

81

in your personal identity. You carve your own route and avoid over-compliance.

'To be authentic is literally to be your own author, to discover your own native energies and desires and then to find your own way of acting on them.'
Warren Bennis, leadership expert

There is no short cut to achieving a strong personal identity. It's a journey of many years and you are already on it. However, you can choose to:

- Stay aware of your journey
- Seek experiences that test and strengthen your identity

PERSONAL EXPERIENCE

You are responsible for your own development and personal growth. No organization can commit enough time or resources to you. The Personnel or Human Resources department will only go so far in providing you with opportunities and training situations. It will never be quite enough.

You need some kind of personal plan to develop yourself and provide you with the kind of personal experience that will make you an effective leader. If you do not make one, probably no one else will. Even if they do, you are the only one really committed to making it work.

You already bring a wealth of personal history to the job of leading. Often this experience may have had little directly to do with actually leading. For example, your ability to understand and empathize with others comes from having shared similar experiences.

If people around you are facing chaos, success, loss, uncertainty, triumph, despair – you are more able to lead them through these periods if you have encountered similar experiences. Our personal history provides us with some rich resources to deal with current problems.

We are also much more than just our history. While past experience has value, in our fast-changing world, it may prevent us from taking a fresh look at what is happening around us. Leaders approach each new situation with an enquiring mind, a readiness to do things differently.

Great leaders abandon old ideas and provide first a shock and then an inspiration for their followers. When Alexander cut the Gordian knot, rather than trying to unravel it, he was refusing to let past experience dictate how he solved the problem. His solution has inspired people ever since. Despite years of imprisonment, Nelson Mandela refused to allow bitterness to colour his approach to dealing with those who had imprisoned him. This transformed the negotiations that eventually led to him becoming President of South Africa. It inspired some of his strongest enemies who came to see him as an acceptable leader.

How can you capitalize on your personal experience? The simplest way is to always conduct a debriefing of every project, big or small. Dissect every failure, not to apportion blame but to answer a simple question:

What can I learn from this?

Study individuals like you who have already mastered the skills you need. It could be running a meeting, giving inspiring presentations, making a sale, conducting an interview. How could you acquire such mastery? What personal experiences will you need to became a master at it too?

PERSONAL STYLE

'To live is not just to survive, but to thrive with passion, compassion, some humour and style.'
Maya Angelou

Style is another factor that distinguishes your way of leading from how others do it. Style is a combination of elements and actions which form a distinct pattern of consistent behaviour. Certainly, a leader's style is usually recognized by others.

Understanding how you come across to other people means exploring both the good and the bad elements of your style. There is your ability to listen, communicate clearly, get things done. Other aspects of your style may be less inspiring, such as your impatience, your lateness for meetings, your loss of the big picture when under pressure and so on.

The strongest part of your style may be something that you least recognize or even value. Perhaps it is your humour or your caring that people find appealing about you as a potential leader. Only if you know and acknowledge these assets can you capitalize on them.

It can be confusing to separate what is your essential style from how people view you in terms of a formal role. So truly effective leaders want feedback from outside sources that see reality. Enlightened kings, for instance, hired advisers and travelling philosophers from foreign lands, or visited them in their own territory.

Today's forward-thinking business leaders visit colleagues in different organizations, use outside consultants and adopt coaches to offer them a different truth from the one readily on the lips of subordinates.

Your personal style provides freedom to be the opposite, without losing yourself. For example, if you are generally pleasant and smiley you have plenty of room to be occasionally tough and uncompromising. Similarly, if you tend to be a rather serious, thoughtful person, you have scope to be exactly the opposite, without being immediately dismissed as frivolous.

PERSONAL VALUES

'Nowadays people know the price of everything and the value of nothing.'
   Oscar Wilde

What comes to mind when someone says Marks and Spencer, Body Shop, IBM, SmithKline Beecham, the BBC, McDonald's? Each of these companies has strong values that influence how we regard them. Their values appear in everything they do and how they do it.

The same goes for leaders. What do you stand for? What do you really care about? What most matters to you? The answers will show up in your work, your possessions and in your relationships. Review all three and see if you can identify the values that matter. Are they of use to other people? Destructive values are unlikely to draw widespread support.

'The trouble with the rat race is that even if you win, you're still a rat.'
   Lily Tomlin

Could you explain your personal values to other people? Everyone knew what Gandhi stood for, while one of the complaints about President Bush was that he apparently had no strongly held beliefs. Business leaders become well known not merely through their commercial successes, but also because they constantly clarify what they stand for, what matters to them.

- Write out your personal credo or what matters to you
- Spend time clarifying your values
- Make values visible by behaving consistently with them

Being consistent with your values is where the phrase 'walk the talk' comes from. It means if you value quality, for instance, then it appears in everything you do; if you value people, you are seen as caring, someone who spends time with them. If you value efficiency, lead the way by being highly efficient yourself.

Having clear and powerful values allows you to bounce back after setbacks. Because you know what you stand for you are not deterred or undermined by failure. Instead you merely use it to learn from and press onwards towards realizing your vision.

The process of getting clear about your values is time-consuming, hard and never really stops. Invent your own ways of focusing on values, making them explicit, sharing them and keeping them high profile.

By talking about your personal values you show you know your own mind. When you are faced with uncertainty or risk, your values enable you to proceed without direction or even approval from someone in authority. When as a leader you successfully share these values with others you begin to help them make decisions and act independently.

Although values may sound a vague concept, people soon understand what you mean and will usually welcome your attempts to clarify them. When you engage in a dialogue about values, people develop a sense of their own and others' positions. The discussions could be about how you value customers, what is the most appropriate return to shareholders, how best to satisfy certain stakeholders and so on.

Talking values helps bring them alive. Your supporters will be filled with energy and enthusiasm if you speak with passion about those values you both share.

INTEGRITY

'Integrity simply means a willingness not to violate one's identity.'
Erich Fromm

Studies of managers confirm that the most frequent characteristic considered as essential for leadership is integrity. That is, leaders are truthful, trustworthy, have character and convictions.

As a leader, personal integrity is doing what you say you will do:

- Uphold agreements
- Honour contracts
- Keep your word

Leaders with low personal integrity constantly break their word. They seldom last or are remembered, except with distaste.

Do people trust you? That is, do they believe that you'll do what you say you'll do, and trust who you are?

This stems from people knowing that you are true to yourself, living your personal values as honestly as possible.

Gone are the days when leaders were meant to be superior beings, high-flown and haughty. These days, leaders need to be seen as real, down-to-earth and fully rounded human beings.

By knowing yourself sufficiently, you become able to accept who you are. It is this honest merging of all aspects of yourself that produces integrity. It is why you appear consistent to others.

'The secret of success is consistency of purpose.'
Benjamin Disraeli

NETWORKS

One 'I' that certainly does not feature in our 7 I's of leadership is *Isolation.* So many leaders succeed because of their personal contacts. They have a huge network of people from whom they draw information and which helps them confirm that they are pursuing their goals efficiently.

Leaders in many organizations are recruited simply because they bring with them a whole list of personal contacts. If you are a start-up entrepreneur, ask yourself, 'Do I personally know a hundred people who would be interested in my product or service?'

Chapter 5 highlights how productive it is to involve as many people as possible in your schemes, gaining you a mass of energetic support. The same goes for your personal network of friends, colleagues and acquaintances.

Building networks does not mean developing relationships just to extract business from them. Nor does it mean manipulating people to advance your career. Respected leaders usually develop these contacts from a genuine desire to make friends with people. Their natural gregariousness and wish to participate, help to generate networking.

Like any relationship you need to work at networking. You cannot ignore someone for years and then expect them to perform favours when you contact them out of the blue. Nurture your contacts, spend time looking after them. Seek opportunities to help them out when you can. Pass on ideas or information if you feel it will support them. The more you put out, the more you will get back.

The 7 I's
of Leadership

✦ **Action-minded**
✦ **Modelling**
✦ **Feedback**
✦ **Perseverance**
✦ **Celebration**

CHAPTER 7

Implementation

What makes some leaders so unstoppable? Typically it is their obsession for making things happen, sometimes at almost any price.

Talk about what you want to achieve – endlessly.

Be willing also to devote apparently limitless energy to ensuring your words are turned into deeds.

'Well done, is better than, well said.'
   Benjamin Franklin

Successful leaders are implementation experts. They are fully aware that rhetoric is only a starting point. To be a leader who implements you:

- Model behaviour
- Are action-minded
- Demand feedback
- Persevere
- Celebrate success

Achieving action is every leader's dream. Modern

leadership requires high credibility because the old-style approach of using power and position to get what you want no longer really works. If you resort to these devices you are not leading, you are dictating.

MODEL BEHAVIOUR

'Example is leadership.'
Albert Schweitzer

Modelling speaks louder than words. It is what 'walk the talk' is about, behaving as you want others to behave. Be the first to demonstrate all the 7 I's. You gain leadership credibility through practising what you preach. When you set an example people believe what you say, and start trying to emulate your example.

Showing through your own actions what you expect is a form of coaching. It conveys more convincingly than exhortations, what you want to happen. It gives you an enormously powerful tool. You cannot lead from behind and expect people to be other than cynical about your leadership.

**Nothing undermines a leader more than suggesting:
'don't do as I do, do as I say'.**

When you lead by example, you become highly visible. Great leaders do not need to be show-offs. They are willing to be seen, and held accountable. There is no hiding as a leader, particularly in an age of rapid change and almost instant communications.

Do you hate public attention and news about how you come across? If so, you will automatically reduce your impact. Successful leaders do not allow their frail egos to prevent them from putting themselves and their ideas into the world. Being a leader is being upfront.

By leading through example you:

- Share your vision
- Promote your values
- Show commitment to achieving results

It is easy to underestimate the power of modelling. Yet it achieves far more than exhortation. Mere words about what you want to achieve, soon bore potential followers into looking elsewhere for inspiration. They want help converting the rhetoric into practical tasks. They need to understand how to play a real part in achieving the vision.

'Leaders must be seen to be upfront, up to date, up to their job and up early in the morning.'
Lord Sieff, former chairman of Marks & Spencer

Modelling, or lack of it, commonly distinguishes managers from true leaders. It is far easier to issue tablets from the mountain than show the way yourself. For example, the failure of many quality initiatives and other such schemes can often be traced back to the reluctance of senior business managers to fully embrace their own message of what they want to happen.

Not believing in something makes modelling it yourself a terrific strain. How can you automatically show what is needed if you are intellectually rather than emotionally committed to it? Even when you really care about what you want to achieve, modelling can be hard to achieve consistently. However, it is an indispensable and eloquent way of getting your message across.

A key area in which to demonstrate modelling is in meetings, where much of your time will be spent. This is where hearts and minds join to get action. How you conduct them sends important messages throughout the entire organization. During them you need to:

- Communicate clearly and succinctly
- Be open to suggestions
- Listen attentively
- Make sure everyone is involved
- Keep a tight hold on time

This kind of behaviour sets the standards for others to follow.

ACTION-MINDED

'Whatever you can do or dream you can, begin it. For boldness has genius, power and magic in it. Begin it now!'
    Goethe

Leaders seldom waste time on witch hunts or on justifying why things have not happened. They are much more concerned with the future, with making something happen. Being action-minded means you:

- Prefer deeds above words
- Make decisions
- Think and communicate with purpose
- Follow-through
- Identify practical tasks
- Ask for help

Deeds

Focus on deeds, rather than rhetoric. Persuasive words are certainly important. Yet ultimately people will say 'Yes, but what do you want us to do?'

Without a strong focus on deeds you risk being seen only as a prophet or visionary, rather than a leader. Leaders have a leaning towards action, usually at the expense of discussion or prolonged debate. However, this tendency is strongly influenced by culture. For instance, one of the strengths of Japanese organizational leadership is that any new action is fully discussed with everyone concerned, almost to the point where nothing gets done at all. In a crisis, this kind of leadership proves weak, as seen by the failure of emergency services to respond adequately to the 1995 earthquake.

'Nothing comes from doing nothing.'
   William Shakespeare

Make decisions

A straight lack of decision taking often explains why leaders fail to achieve action. However, effective leaders prefer to ensure that those responsible for implementing decisions make them. Your job is to make sure they want to make the decisions and to bear the consequences of them.

Two key actions you can take in this area are to ensure that people have:

- The necessary information on which to base decisions
- Adequate training to recognize when a decision is needed
- The ability to distinguish a good decision from a bad one
- A desire to learn from past decisions

Inexperienced leaders wonder what people will think of them and their performance if they do not personally keep making decisions and giving answers. Typically the reaction is 'I'll lose their respect' or 'I won't be seen as earning my salary'. If people are busy enjoying their jobs they don't in fact think these things and realize that an effective leader is there to serve them, to help them do their own work better.

Once it is clear that it is down to you to make a decision, be willing to take time to reflect, to avoid being pressured into the wrong choice – but set a definite limit for when you must decide. While it is important to weigh up alternatives and see every side of an issue, this is no substitute for the act of making a decision.

'It all comes down to decisiveness. You can use the fanciest computers in the world and you can gather all the charts and numbers, but in the end you have to bring all your information together, set a timetable, and act.'
Lee Iacocca

Think and communicate with purpose

Creative thinking is an important stimulus and source of leadership action. The point about such thinking is that it deals with newness, the future, and with challenging the ways things are always done.

Monitor your own creative thinking by noticing:

- Are my thoughts mainly focused on action?
- Do I prefer rehearsing history, rather than focusing on the future?
- Am I willing to question the 'rules' or rock the boat?

To break the pattern of uncreative thinking, you may

need to do things differently from how you do them at present. For instance, try keeping a notebook or recorder by your bedside. Practise translating your random thoughts and reflections into specific steps for achieving action by asking yourself:

'How could we do that, if necessary?'

Much the same applies to your conversations. Take an interest in how much of your daily communications contain a purpose that demands action, rather than just discussion. Keep a check for a week or so to monitor how much you bemoan what's wrong or attempt to justify mistakes. Leaders avoid such unproductive behaviour.

Follow-through
Golfers and tennis players put full power into a shot by allowing the swing to follow through, *after* hitting the ball. This seems odd. How on earth can hitting it well be affected by what you do afterwards? It's because contact with the ball is only part of an effective action.

All actions have a wider context. In your case they are part of your broader vision. The golfer uses a mental picture of hitting the ball to a certain place and physical follow-through of the swing helps get it there. Likewise, your own vision for your team or organization requires certain actions or follow-through *en route*.

Follow-through by an action-minded leader is full of questions such as:

- 'How are things going?'
- 'What is happening?'
- 'What's the news?'
- 'Tell me the latest'
- 'Give me an update'

The greater the degree of follow-through, the more powerful you make the associated actions. For example, keep asking people what happened after we talked, made a decision, started that project, hired that new person. Do it in an interested way, rather than pestering them, or making them feel you are checking up on them.

Often leaders invent opportunities where others have only seen information or facts. The difference is their determination to stay action-minded, rather than become over-immersed in just data.

Completion

The world is full of people with half-finished projects and ideas that never quite happen. Leaders:

- follow through to completion, or
- formally abandon a possible course of action

When you follow through to completion, you leave more scope to move on and create something else. Typical forms of completion include:

- Doing what you say you'll do
- Tying up the loose ends of projects or tasks
- Phoning people back

Occasionally you cannot complete an action, or conclude it is no longer appropriate. Be sure that you really do abandon it and move on. Uncompleted projects, tasks, paperwork, can all sap your energy, simply through still hanging around, seemingly demanding your attention.

- List ALL your current uncompleted activities or projects

- Set definite deadlines for finishing them
- Identify any areas of your work that are filled with irrelevancies
- Check your physical work space and remove unnecessary clutter

The more you can clear space in your environment and your life, the more you enable new opportunities to enter.

Practical tasks

You will need to go beyond offering a broad statement of intent or vision to create specific, tangible targets. You will be inspiring if you use your personal creativity to invent ways to make these relevant to people, so that they appeal emotionally and also logically.

Set out to show people just *how* an exciting or challenging goal might be achieved. This is being a coach, a mentor and an adviser to your supporters. You may require lots of practice at learning how to convert goals into practical small steps for people to follow. It also means you:

- Ask people for their help
- Apply common sense

Smart goals

A particularly useful way to identify practical actions is the SMART goal system. There are various versions of this acronym. Having tried them out, our preference is a SMART goal which is:

- Stretching – your reach should exceed your grasp; unchallenging goals seldom work
- Measurable – making goals specific so you know whether or not they are achieved and at what rate

- Agreed – ensuring goals are realistic and that people buy into them, not just imposing them
- Recorded – keeping track of events so that you know what is supposed to be achieved and by whom
- Time limited – putting a time boundary around the aim so that people are working to understandable deadlines

Asking for help

Leaders don't do it alone. They are intensely aware that they need supporters. Observe a talented leader and you might wonder whether they have any talent at all. They seem to need so much help! They keep asking everyone around them for it.

For some people asking for help is difficult. Why is it that men drivers who are lost hate asking for directions while women are always happy to do so? Many traditional managers baulk at the idea of revealing they don't have the answers. Successful leaders, though, are less precious about admitting they need help to implement their dreams.

Balance

While it is essential to focus on action as a leader, beware of:

- A manic demand for constant activity
- Losing the big picture

There is a difference between leadership energy and frenetic activity where you never seem to sit still. This is a sign of someone trying to do it all themselves. Leaders who do too much lead for only a short time before they burn out.

Demand feedback

Leaders become experts at both giving and receiving feedback. They refuse to do without it and are tenacious at maintaining it – both ways. The only means of knowing how you are performing as a leader is to obtain feedback. Remaining open to being judged by others is a tough yet essential leadership habit.

The faster a car goes, the greater the wind resistance. Similarly, the more action you take the more 'flak' you are likely to attract. You are bound to meet some objections to your plans, hit natural resistance, face disbelief or incomprehension.

Feedback tells you about these reactions so that you respond appropriately. Both negative and positive are essential for implementing your vision.

Feedback only really makes sense in relation to some goal. Goals alone are harder to achieve without regular feedback on progress towards them. So you need both.

You can give and receive regular feedback in many ways:

- Informal conversations
- Formal sessions such as performance reviews
- Coaching
- Mentoring

Informal conversations

Successful leaders build personal networks to ensure that they receive information from a diversity of sources. For instance, you might ask colleagues: 'How did I do in that meeting?', 'What could I have done that would have been more effective?' 'What worked about what I just did?'

Informal feedback opportunities are everywhere, you just have to take advantage of them. Even a chat in a lift may yield precious data about how you are performing or the progress of your plans.

Formal
Within most organizations there are usually several types of formal mechanisms for obtaining feedback. For example, nowadays leaders can learn about their performance through upward appraisal and 360-degree feedback.

As a leader, ensure that there are formal feedback mechanisms available to serve both you and your supporters. The latter need feedback to know how they are doing and improve. The days of blind obedience to the leader are rapidly disappearing.

Coaching
Who do you turn to for support? You can expect some help from those you lead. However, avoid 'dumping' on them your personal troubles, fears and worries about what you are trying to achieve.

It can be lonely being a leader. Consider finding a coach who offers a fresh perspective to your work, someone who understands that what matters to you is achieving your vision.

Your coach need not be someone within the organization, or even someone who knows a great deal about your business or job. They just need to be someone you respect, who is able to bring different ideas, information and experience to the discussion.

Mentoring
Leaders occasionally find it useful to have more than just a coach, someone whom they admire as modelling how the job should be done. Your mentor might be another leader in an entirely different industry, or even a different part of the world. You may only see the mentor

occasionally, but he or she is available to you for advice and help.

It is not a sign of weakness to adopt a mentor. It shows you are open to new ideas, to developing yourself, and learning from somebody who perhaps has more experience than you. Finding the right mentor is never entirely easy. Think about people you really admire and respect. Are they possible mentors?

Mentors are not meant to give you direction, or solve your problems with a simple answer. They are a sounding board, a resource to stimulate you and share some of the difficulties of the leadership role.

PERSEVERANCE

'*Victory belongs to the most persevering.*'
    Napoleon

In the film *Forest Gump*, the hero's endless dash across America eventually attracts a dedicated band of followers attracted by his perseverance. They don't even know exactly why he's running, only that he never seems to stop. Sheer persistence often sets leaders apart from other people. They continue long after others have given up, abandoned hope or lost enthusiasm. This persistence eventually becomes a source of inspiration.

Credible leaders keep hope alive. They sustain it with their determination, and higher aspirations. Fostering realistic yet optimistic attitudes, helps people accept more challenging goals and achievements.

Perseverance comes from a deep belief in what you want to achieve. The more clear you are about this the more likely that others will find your persistence attractive. By not easily giving up, leaders overcome obstacles that at first sight might seem impossible.

The whole point of having support, involving others and creating networks is that it is hard to keep going sometimes. While the more passionate you are about your vision the more likely you are to achieve it, there will always be moments of self-doubt, or concern about the obstacles. During these times you dig deep inside yourself to find that extra bit of commitment to persist.

Dogged determination is not something you can learn – but you can practise it. This is when you need to tap those personal sources of inspiration mentioned earlier.

'Diamonds are only chunks of coal, that stuck to their jobs, you see'
Minnie Richards Smith

CELEBRATION

It is important to pat yourself on the back when things are going well, not just when you achieve your final goal. By regularly celebrating small achievements that add up to a big one, you give yourself and others inspiration to continue.

Achievement deserves reward. If you have the right team, they will probably be the first to congratulate you. Sometimes, though, others are unaware of what you have achieved. As leader you may be the only one to appreciate the nature of the triumph fully and be able to celebrate it. So treat yourself!

It is equally vital to celebrate other people's successes. Sometimes simply turning up and showing that you care about what they have achieved is sufficient to make an impact. Make sure you know when people have triumphed and model celebratory behaviour.

Grab opportunities to celebrate success without waiting for the formal opportunities to underline it. For example, if you think people have done something exceptional, rather than waiting for a grand occasion to say so, consider giving everyone the day off then and there so you can all go somewhere exciting to celebrate.

By breaking goals into manageable steps, you provide milestones where supporters can, in effect, pause and admire the view. Ask them to help identify these and how they would like to celebrate reaching each one.

Find ways of identifying corporate achievement – end-of-year figures, new contracts, faultless administration, quality production, exceptional customer feedback – and celebrate these. When you start to take these kinds of achievements for granted you will be starting to diminish your leadership impact.

You will find your own appropriate style to encourage celebrations. While it may not be razzmatazz, people do need to know what success feels like. It makes them hungry for more.

AND FINALLY

The 7 I's of leadership: Insight, Initiative, Inspiration, Involvement, Improvisation, Individuality, and Implementation can help you to achieve your vision.

Leadership is not an easy burden although it is a vital one. The world needs leaders. Our planet and the people who live here are in dire need of people who have the imagination and inspiration to help create a better world. You personally can make a difference. There are a lot of people out there waiting for you.

'Our deepest fear is not that we are inadequate. Our deepest fear is that we are powerful beyond measure. It is our light, not our darkness that most frightens us. As we let our own light shine, we unconsciously give other people permission to do the same. As we are liberated from our own fear, our presence automatically liberates others.'

Nelson Mandela, 1994 Inaugural Speech

The 7 I's of Leadership

+ Self-awareness
+ Understanding others
+ Seeing the situation

+ Taking responsibility
+ Risk
+ Direct action
+ Vitality

+ Vision
+ Communication
+ Passion
+ Trust

+ Enrolment
+ Empowerment
+ Personal investment
+ Feedback
+ Stakeholders

+ Creativity
+ Flexibility
+ Presence

+ Being yourself
+ Personal experience
+ Style
+ Values
+ Integrity
+ Networking

+ Action-minded
+ Modelling
+ Feedback
+ Perseverance
+ Celebration

Leadership is in the I of the beholder